BOOK REVIEWS OF
Fadwa Tuqan, Love Letters to Sami Haddad

Fadwa Tuqan, an eminent Palestinian poet, relies on love to help her transcend the injustices of life: the Israeli occupation of her beloved land, loneliness, and pain. However, her *Love Letters to Sami Haddad* are about the power of love, how such love gives the person wings to fly beyond misery, and how she, Fadwa, through love transcended the world that was collapsing around her.

Dr. May Rihani
served as
Director of the Chair of Gibran for Values and Peace at the University of Maryland

There remains an urgent need to read *Fadwa Tuqan, Love Letters to Sami Haddad* as it illuminates an important aspect in the life of the preeminent Palestinian poet, Fadwa Tuqan, on one hand. On the other hand, it clarifies the nature of a dark stage that the Palestinian cause suffered as Fadwa Tuqan sensitively pens the June setback and its aftermath in dark colors. It is not surprising that these letters seem like elaborate prose poems replete with poetic images and the true feelings of a creative poet who endured this infliction by the occupation of her homeland. This is the case of all Palestinians, whether in the occupied land or as expatriates living by force as strangers far from their land and the land of their fathers and grandfathers.

Dr. Sabry Hammadi
Professor of Arabic in the Department of Foreign Languages, Washtenaw College, Ann Arbor, Michigan, USA;
Former Professor of Modern Literature at the University of Mosul;
Professor of Contemporary Literary Criticism and former Dean at the University of Dhamar, Yemen

This compiled series of 24 love letters sent in the mid-1970's by Fadwa Tuqan in Palestine to Sami Haddad in London is a poignant description of life in Palestine under Israeli occupation. Between the lines and behind the expressions of love, the reader feels the will of the Palestinians for resistance against the occupation. A book worth reading.

Ambassador (Ret.) Massoud Maalouf
Lebanese Ambassador to Canada

Fadwa Tuqan

Love Letters

to Sami Haddad

Prepared for Publication by Samir Haddad

Review and Introduction by Abdul-Latif Alwarari

Translated from the Arabic by Reem M. Nuseibeh

Fadwa Tuqan

Love Letters

to Sami Haddad

First Printing – November 2023
Second Printing – March 2024

ISBN: 978-0-9968933-9-8 *(paperback)*

Printed in the United States of America on acid-free paper.

Published by Mosaic Design Book Publishers

Dearborn, Michigan USA

0 1 2 3 4 5 6 7 8 9

Love Letters
to Sami Haddad

Fadwa Tuqan (1917 – 2003) is one of the most important Palestinian poets in the twentieth century. She was born in the city of Nablus to a well-known Palestinian family. She was called the Poet of Palestine, as her poetry represented a strong foundation for female experiences in love, revolution, and women's protest against society.

Sami Haddad (1939 – 2021) was a Jordanian broadcaster and one of the oldest broadcasters on BBC Radio, then on Al-Jazeera, where he presented, from the mid-1990s to November 2009, the program "More than an Opinion". He has an unpublished collection of poetry.

Table of Contents

"The oath I have taken with you makes me love you even more.
Yet here I am, on alert. I lost the gift of love years ago.
I see you laughing, and I am so delighted to watch you.
I have two remaining talents – poetry and
my passionate love for the land."

Fadwa Tuqan

Introduction

1. **Letters of … Real Love:**

These are new, previously unpublished letters by Palestinian poet Fadwa Tuqan (1917-2003). Their release follows the publication of letters she exchanged with Thurayya Haddad two years ago.[1] They are love letters in the real sense of the word. At times, they are abundant with nobility and imbued with a sense of giving, and, at other times, rife with turmoil of life's darker side.

As the poet writes these letters, she entrusts them with the secrets of her deep passion and eloquent love, and the process resurrects her. It is as though these letters rekindle the memory of a time long ago in her life. She lived a real love story, in addition to the one she enjoyed through her correspondence with Egyptian writer, Anwar Al-Ma'adawi, as we learned from the well-known exchange between Jubran and May Ziyadeh.

Fadwa and Al-Ma'adawi – as Rajaa' Al-Naqqash argues – never met in person. Instead, they realized mutual satisfaction by exchanging letters and poems about that love[2], even though Fadwa acknowledged later that there was true love between them and that she had expressed this love in more than one poem[3].

However, the love she addresses in these letters and about which she writes with such burning passion and delight simultaneously is a real love experienced with her all senses between herself and the Palestinian-Jordanian writer and media personality, Sami Haddad.[4]

---

1. *Fadwa Tuqan's Letters to Thurayya Haddad* (New Light on Her Life and Poetry), reviewed and presented by Abdul Lateef Al Warari and prepared for publication by Samir Haddad, Tibaq Publishing House, Ramallah, Palestine, First Edition, 2018.
2. Rajaa' Al-Naqqash, Between Al-Ma'addawi and Fadwa Tuqan are Unknown Pages in Contemporary Arab Literature, Dar Al-Marreekh, Al-Riyadh, Second Edition, 1410 AH/1990 AD, page 27.
3. Ibid, page 13.
4. Sami was reluctant to open the box of letters after all this time as he had almost forgotten the whole thing, until his brother, the esteemed media personality Samir Haddad, managed to convince him to open the box and send the letters to him for publication.

This love story began in 1975, when Fadwa visited England. There she met Sami and was delighted to get to know him, as she herself concedes in her first letter. Their relationship grew stronger, when Fadwa helped Sami prepare his thesis about the well-known popular Jordanian poet, Nimer Al-Udwan. Fadwa mediated with the poet's family to collect his written poems. As she wrote to Sami, "I will be very happy to do anything to help you in this regard." Indeed, she was keen on keeping her promise to communicate with the poet's family about Nimer's poems, and she did so with great pleasure. Even though Fadwa and Sami had known each other for a short time, she felt like she had known him for many years, as evidenced by her sense of loneliness at the time, and of which she reminded him from time to time.

Once Fadwa grew comfortable in the relationship and love grew stronger between them, she was not afraid to disclose and express her feelings that remained unchanged under the unjust Zionist occupation of her homeland Palestine. She suffered alongside her own people from collective punishment, such as the closure of the Allenby Bridge, from excessive curiosity from postal workers as she mailed her letters, and from the occupation soldiers as well.[5] As the days seemed to look the same, she saw only the dark side of everything in that world, as the deluge of the khaki-clad military flooded the sidewalks every Saturday – the official sabbath in Israel – when Israelis flocked to her occupied city and roamed its streets under the protection of the occupation soldiers, further deepening her sense of alienation in her occupied homeland. In one of her letters, we can almost hear her scream poetically, "Here I am, O Sami, taking a scoop from the river of time/ who will save me, who will save me from this death?"

2. Letters as an Antidote

However, this budding love, so important for someone at her age and unfortunate lot, soon became enriched with poetry, art, and music through her exchange of love letters and postcards; through

---

5. Poet Fadwa Tuqan states in one of her letters that on her way back from a summer vacation, a Jewish lieutenant on the bridge seized one of her poems and read it with curiosity. She wrote: "I left the room cursing these horrible times and wondering bitterly 'if human beings were created to fall into the trap of a world dominated by evil and wanton.'"

nooks and new poems; or by way of songs and poetry recordings aired on the BBC radio, including the show, *Morning Thoughts*, for which Fadwa presented poetry for a month. Their budding love also manifested in theatrical and art shows that she and Sami attended on her visits to London. "For me, there's nothing more beautiful in life than meeting a human being with the soul of a poet, and I have discovered this poet in you as you read your poems to me on that summer evening in London."

From Nablus to London and vice versa, their letters serve as an antidote, a bridge of live emotions. Fadwa receives Sami's letters with open arms, as her soul finds solace in the warmth of her flowing emotions. She would respond the next day or the day after, "when I would collect parts of myself scattered here and there." Fadwa does not write her letters in hasty response, as it becomes more obvious; rather writing depends on her mood and the timing of her heart. For that reason, we gain sincere intellectual and artistic knowledge from her letters that carry her personal imprint, all the while keeping a mental aesthetic distance from them. She does not elaborate in her letters, as agreed, and remains cautious how she expresses her creative clarity. Sometimes, she even decides to stop, given her well-known penchant for privacy and aloof nature. At other times, however, the overflow of "the rain pouring out of the horizon of the heart and soul" overtakes her. Love is her steering wheel, and her love letters mean that she opens the balcony door and overcomes the "frost of loneliness" that she experienced in her solitude. Was it not for this bridge that she extended to the one she loved and to whom she exchanged the true emotions of her private life.

Over the BBC radio, she found another antidote in the voice of her beloved, as she woke up early every day to listen in to the programs he presented (This Morning), taking her on a journey through museums, lecture halls, and Oriental music concerts over the ether, letting the vibration of the radio waves fill her heart with joy. She writes: "In *This Morning* episode, you presented today (…), I felt you at the very core of my emotions. It's true my feelings for you are permanent; however, sometimes they have an authoritarian and dominating flare."

For that reason, she eagerly waited for him every morning, complaining if he was a bit fake, if the effects of a cold appeared to affect him visibly. She even worried if he was went missing for a while and was absent of her morning show for some time: "If your voice was missing from my horizon, who will recharge the bleak days with light and warmth?"

The music over the airwaves also felt like magic touched Fadwa's emotions, especially when old songs brought back hidden memories or transported those of Jubilee, the London neighborhood that witnessed their love, and memories would flow through her mind.

From letters to radio airwaves, whenever the poet's emptiness intensified, she which transform the bridges of separation into actual physical meetings, for the spiritual connection no longer satisfied her or quenched her thirst to meet her beloved once again in London or in Nablus where she expected him to make good on his promises to visit, before these expectations would disappear into thin air.

3. **From the Joy of Meeting to the Gravity of Absence:**

Fadwa was sincere about his love and for her love. She describes this love as working on the "timing of eternity." She did not utter a single word that would stir the calmness of its beautiful waters, until a sudden "healing wound" opened again, making her believe that all beautiful things in her life are suffering, and even "the face of the world was being distorted." A "third person" called (Yaju) surfaced and started to harm things at the core.

This created in her soul the well-known "Hamiltonian" hesitation, so she became suspicious at times and ambivalent and cynical at other times about a strange world rife with contradictions. Her relationship between the love letters that she so openly and sincerely penned and the recipient himself worsened.[6] This prevented her from baring her soul in her correspondence, but without uttering a

6. Fadwa used to hint at that to Sami, but she openly disclosed her feelings in a letter she wrote to his sister Thurayya Haddad on September 2, 1977: "Sami has killed all beautiful things, and I am certain, after getting to know him well, that he possesses the talent of destroying things, even if maintaining these things takes minimum effort or sacrifice."

single bad word or acting in an ugly selfishness. Rather, she rather elevated herself above all that was happening and all hearsay and gossip with utmost self-control and poise.

Even though this situation caused her pain and internal bleeding, she wisely masked it so as not to spoil the sweetness of the story she lived or her relationship with the loved one, opting to let things flow freely without any complication. However, that plunged her into an emotional contradiction between her overjoy about the loved one and her strong yearning for the missing distant beloved.

She likened herself, as silence and the vacuum started to spread through the relationship, to the legendary Goddess Madea; however, unlike her, she would not inflict pain on others but rather hurt herself to please others, making her feeling lost. She would continue to search for herself in the desert, all alone in silence and perplexity, before getting used to the arid rocky terrain, gaining a wealth of experience in the process.

The dreamy love story instantly turned into a laughable comedy and then into a tragedy that doomed the entire affair to end, save for the vivid colorful memories. "The unjustifiable bleak ending to our beautiful friendship was a source of sadness to me, for everything seemed to be perfect, based on mutual understanding and harmony, and then, without any introduction, life between us turned motionless."

The longest of all the other letters is due to its symbolic lucidity, memory-based nature, and stream of consciousness. Fadwa talks about this eloquent lesson which is: "our ability to love!" In this letter, she recalls the story of a friend of hers since childhood. However, this friend was none other than Fadwa herself. The sincere and spontaneous Fadwa, the Fadwa whose words are nothing but a mere reflection of her real and deep emotions, the Fadwa in love who possessed an amazing emotional dynamic before the June 1967 war. Fadwa is eternally occupied with love before turning into a Chekhov character, tormented with conflicting unexplainable emotions, before she becomes the legendary Madea and the Nablus girl. On her solemn face shines a teardrop, driven by a powerful undercurrent into a poet whose imagination and reactions cut her off from the outside world, yet she tries to learn and to earn this love and deserve life, despite her tremendous difficulties.

"Our ability to love!" That is everything and whatever remains are just details in the core of the human story.

But what could she do in front of the mirror when time has shattered it into pieces, while her heart remained on fire? Ibn Zahr of Seville best described her situation:

> I stood before the mirror to ask it
> and my eyelids denied everything they saw
> I asked where is that person who stood here yesterday
> When did this person depart and how?
> The mirror mocked me and said without a word being uttered
> That was then and after that, this is what followed!

4. **Career Concerns**

Poet Fadwa Tuqan included important aspects of her career, poetry, and positions vis a vis existence, making these letters ever more valuable.

Looking at these letters all the way back to the mid-1970s (75, 76 and 77)[7], Fadwa was feeling the "dizziness" that was encroaching on her private and public life, for she condemned the Israeli occupation and the oppression and usurpation it imposed, as well as the complacent Arab era stifled under the yoke of endless, incessant conspiracies to suck the strength of her Arab nation. She stood in amazement about what was happening around her, seeking in vain to make sense of all of it. She saw those conspiring against the Palestine question disrupting the forward movement started by the October 1973 war, inflicting more harm on her than Israel has ever done. It as though it was her destiny and the destiny of her entire generation to be "the generation of pain, crucifixion and turmoil."

---

7. Even though the letters continued in one form or another and in a new context between Fadwa and Thurayya at the end of the 1970s with the specter of Sami in the background.

Her own conclusions revealed that the political experience had its own ebb and flow at the time, and that the whole region, plunged into endless darkness, was standing on shifting sands. What was her prediction?

She did not hide her concern and pessimism. In spite of that, she took a stronger stand than her nature allowed and from the "inevitability of nature" as she recalled her optimism, hoping that she would live longer to share the happiness of her fighting people. The "will of living is strongest, or else what is the meaning of this continued struggle between the forces of darkness and a people who insist on living and refusing to surrender? This struggle could be prolonged and could last two generations or three or more."

As such, she was a dreamer poet and fighter. She does not hesitate to shake with her poems the "Virgin Mary" tree the dates and fruits of which her people deserve. Out of concern for the future of her people, she reads books about the cause of her people, such as *The Palestine Question and Projects for Political Solutions*. She held poetry readings throughout the West Bank, including a lecture, "Palestinian Poetry," she presented at Umm Al-Fahm Youth Club, to keep the youth in touch with the poets of Palestine and the poetry before 1948 as a result of being disconnected from Arab thought under the occupation. But one cannot be separate from their roots, like an Arab living in Europe, feeling lost and remorseful but not losing their roots, regardless of how long they were away from their homeland. The roots remain firmly planted in the distant land, glistening under the sun and the palm trees.

She is saddened by the Arabs remaining Kantian and mired in the abyss of poverty, ignorance, and disease, instead of overcoming the past toward a present and a future that celebrates a fertile contribution to civilization, much like their forefathers did in ancient times. She feels sad, too, by some classes' exploitation of religion for their own narrow interests and whims to "seize the reigns of miserable Islamic nations and control their resources." She declares her objection to this "political" religion, an exploitation tool for a specific class of people, to the point that she wishes to see "communism sweep all Arab oil producing countries."

The political reality and the general atmosphere affects her personal life and hurts without limit. So do the daily concerns of her close relatives: "And why do I carry the concerns of other people?" and "Does anyone feel my pain? I have suffered alone my entire life; I suffered alone, felt sad and pain alone without anyone near or far sharing the burden. But what can I do about this soul that feels tormented by the misery of other people?"

She tries in vain to find a way to reconcile with herself and to follow her personal compass to restore harmony and peace; for "internal conflict only subsides with death," as she screams out in a moment of self-revelation: "What lightning struck the forests of the self and set them on fire!"

Our poet's soul appears to have fallen under the siege of reality and other people's concerns to the point of suffocation, yearning for absolute solitude with her favorite books and to writing, writing, writing. She traveled to Jericho where, for restless nights under God's palm tree, she would dive into the world of Chekhov and his convoluted human psychology, as though she found in it the consolation and energy she had been missing. She adored nighttime and loved to listen to Andalusian music and ballads that hearkened back to her childhood, allowing her to relive "long gone years that would never return." She did not like western music, save for some symphonies, and she sometimes found refuge in isolation, writing about "solutions and the void" and yearnings that came out into the open out of nowhere.

Literature, art, poetry, and music fueled her soul with richness and joy, and the spring delved into her political interests, thoughts, and subjects.

No letter was devoid of poetry and talk about poetry, for she was possessed with it; she yearned for it like water and air. But what concerns us is her mood while writing a poem, the rituals of writing, and her psychological motives, for she does not write according to a tribal vision. Instead, she allows her instantaneous reactions to steer her poems away from where she started: "When I first start writing poetry, I believed that I will continue to recall memories of days long gone, from the days of patience, poetry and love; but I find myself down a different path." Her own spontaneity in writing poetry leads her, unless she becomes impeded "under the yoke of emotional duality and contradiction." And rather than approve the final form of a poem, she would edit it, add or delete, or make changes to it. "I made some changes to the last poem about Jericho. I usually leave the poem after finishing it and go back to it after I have acquired a new time perspective and make changes here and there."

Only then does a poem achieve a grand worship ritual: "When I sat down yesterday evening with my pen and papers to write back to you, I found myself feeling the birth of a poem inside of me, and as usual, I froze, still in the chair behind the desk and started daydreaming. You should have seen your friend deep in thought about poetry. You would have mistaken her for an Indian priest lost in mediation."

These letters are a reflection of her existence and living testimony to the existence of an influential poet like Fadwa Tuqan and her true love that combines her fragility and sensitivity, and at the same time, the age and surroundings that teem with events, lies, and collective loss. As such, it is unacceptable for these letters to remain hidden in the drawers of oblivion.

Nothing in any of these letters defiles Fadwa or undermines her great iconic personality. Rather, they strengthen our great pride in her and our yearning to listen to her voice once again, thus rediscovering new details of her personal and emotional life and her poetic style.

I organized the letters chronologically between 1975 and 1977, and I was mindful of the common thread between them, like the plot of a unique story. I also gave these letters headlines, and under each headline, I included a sentence extracted from the respective letter in a very telling manner, without letting my own curiosity inject myself into them.

1. If I Could Do Anything for You

"... for there's nothing more beautiful than meeting good people – especially poets – for a person to feel richer and more complete with their love and their friendship."

Nablus, July 28, 1975

My dearest friend Sami,
Warm regards and greetings

I returned to Amman and stopped by the house of my dear brother and friend Sulaiman to thank him for giving you my poem which is a way for us to get to know each more closely. There's nothing more beautiful than that of meeting kind people – especially poets – to feel more enriched with their love and friendship. The truth is I came back from London feeling delighted to have met you and to have become acquainted with the (poet) in you.

As soon as I arrived in Nablus, I immediately contacted Mr. Ihsan Al-Nimer and visited him last night. We discussed the letter you are preparing about poet Nimer Al-Udwan, and when I asked him about the poems he has, he retrieved a large notebook, or what he calls "Ihsan Al-Nimer's Record," only to find that it contained only two poems, and neither was new to me. One of them starts with this verse:

"O Uqab, I begin my complaint from two issues:
Suffering and separation from my beloved, whom I want back."

He recited it on the night before the Eid. As for the second poem, he recited it on the day Wadha took his mare to the water to drink.

"I remembered O God at the water spring,
O God, protect me from her envious eyes."

And even though I am almost certain that you do not need Nimr Al-Udwan's two well-known verses of poetry, I decided to copy them from his notebook and forward them to you in the hope they would be of good use to you.

As for the two hundred poems that the author referred to in his book on the history of Nablus, the story was relayed by Sheikh Saleh Al-Khafsh, who memorized Al-Udwan's poetry. If you refer to the second part of "Jabal Nablus," page 482, you will find the following written in the footnote:

(Sheikh Saleh Al-Khafsh told me: I have entered two hundred of Nimr Al-Udwan's poems, and I have memorized one hundred twenty of these poems, etc.)

Thus, I found myself not gaining much from meeting Ihsan Al-Nimr, save for these two poems. However, I contacted Sheikh Al-Khafsh's grandchildren and asked if they kept any of their grandfather's papers. They informed me that they had some notebooks here and there, including some in Kuwait that his children kept, and they promised to collect whatever they could gather from his notebooks and let me look at them. Since you were waiting to hear from me in this regard, I wanted to write these quick words to update you after reviewing Al-Khafsh's notebooks, hoping to provide you with some useful information. I will be happy to do anything that would assist you in this regard.

Hoping you would receive this letter in good health and wishing you the best. God bless you.

Fadwa Tuqan

2. Sequels of the Valley of the Abyss

"My life has not changed
The days are all the same – nights followed by dawn –
I dream, I work, I wait for the dawn to rise …
All my days are the same, except for Saturday."

This letter is to be read on the beats of "The Rectifier"
Occupied Nablus
August 1975
Noon, Saturday

Dearest Sami,
I received a letter from you today. It contained a pulse/poetry:

Your words are budding, blossoming, taking me back to the days long gone,
Making me forget these restless times, the times of oppression,
I sniff the whiff of amber and seek shelter from the sun in the shade of green trees.

Sami dearest,

Nothing has changed in my life.
My days are all the same – nights followed by dawn.
I dream, work, wait for the crack of dawn…

My days are all the same, except for Saturday.

If you knew what Saturdays mean to me:
Things here in my country take on a dark side and have an unbearable smell and
O the taste, it makes colocynth taste sweet!
Patience leaves my heart on Saturdays.
As this flood of "khakis" sweeps the sidewalks,
Soldiers scattered here and there block my arteries,
Drowning me in humiliation and subjugation,
Growing in my body a tree of hate.
My throat clogs up to death, and I am unable to swallow on Saturdays.

Had Nimr Al-Udwan seen me on Saturdays, he would have dedicated a poem to me under the title "Wadha has died once."

He would drink the cup of death a thousand times a day/
I hate them, how much I hate Saturdays/
I take them with the arrows of rejection and the sighs of a wounded heart
And I move forward in spite of my suffering as I boldly sigh:
O my homeland, O my homeland!
As I squeeze the fruits of colocynth in these bitter words,
I am taken aback by the sound of the radio penetrating my silence,
announcing the news summary/

This is the voice of "Nadeem." Rather, this is the voice of "Qusay." But why does he sound so "confused"?

There's something amiss in his voice/
I listen closely. What, what?

On the first Monday of September,
The president will meet with Kissinger and will sign ....
My pain, O my pain/
Here I am falling into the trap.../
Here I am, O Sami, scooping from the river of time,
Who will save me?
Who will rescue me from this death?

My will: O Sami, goodbye/
They dug me a grave in a valley called the Valley of the Abyss/
I am preparing for death/
And I asked God to grant me forgiveness/
And if you happen to visit my grave one day
And if you pray for my soul,
Just read "Al-Fatiha" of oil!

Yours truly
Fadwa Tuqan

3. Manuscript of Al-Udwan's Poetry

"I miss you, and I thank you profusely for your beautiful attention to broadcasting interviews ..."

Nablus, September 1, 1975

O Dear Sami,

Just a quick word to relay good news about the poems of Nimr Al-Udwan that have recently come into my possession after waiting patiently for the grandchildren of Sheikh Al-Khafsh who did not have enough time to deliver them to me much sooner.

In any case, I am thankful to them. I promise you that I will copy these poems quickly and forward them to you on a firsthand basis. There are not as many poems as Ihsan Al-Nimr had indicated, but they do contain poems by other Bedouin poets with whom Al-Nimr exchanged duos. I will forward these poems to you, given their relevance to the subject at hand. I only hope you would find them useful to your research study. I wish I could have sent you the whole collection, but the Al-Khafsh family are keen to protect this inheritance as a valuable treasure.

I just had an idea. I will try to talk them into sending the entire manuscript to you, telling them this would be to commemorate their grandfather in the service of science, ideology, and knowledge.

I miss you. Thank you very much for your keen interest in broadcasting the interviews and for sending the telegram that you had promised me. It had the biggest impact on me today, and after I deposit this letter in the mailbox today, I will stop to see the grandchildren of Al-Khafsh and propose my idea. If they agree, I will take the manuscripts to Amman and send them to you with any friend or family who might be traveling to you. If they refuse, I will copy them as I mentioned earlier.

Please send my regards to your beautiful Italian (female) friend, and please be safe. Blessings.

Yours truly
Fadwa Tuqan

4. Old Songs

"Old songs take me back to the early days of my childhood, when I was quietly enamored with the loving voice of my mother as she sang those songs . . ."

Nablus, September 4, 1975

Dearest Sami,

This is a quick follow up to my last letter. I have photocopied the poems of Nimr Al-Udwan, and I have learned that our dear friend Qusay will be visiting us this month. At that time, I will give him the photocopied poems to give to you.

For my reward, you must recite to me the Andalusian poetry of Sayyed Darwish sung by Fairuz.

Old songs take me back to the early days of my childhood, when I was quietly enamored with the loving voice of my mother as she sang those old songs. They also take me back to the distant past, when I held the "leadership" position among my sisters, my mother, and some of my brothers – especially Ibrahim – when I played music and we all sang like a chorus, when we knew that my cousins and father were out of the house, as singing like that was forbidden…

I remembered a poem by Robert Browning telling how great old songs are and how they rekindle memories and evoke all kinds of emotions, beautiful yet painful emotions. Thus these songs make us relive long lost years, and through the feelings joy and misery, we remember one picture after the other.

I can't help it. I find myself feeling comfortable talking to you, but I will let you go now in God's peace.

Lots of love.

5. Love in the Age of Occupation

"I am possessed by the occupation; it is an inescapable thought, and where can I run or hide?"

Nablus, September 20, 1975

O Dearest Sami,

Two weeks ago, I posted my last letter to you about Nimr Al-Udwan's letters. Before leaving the post office, I checked my mailbox to find your letter waiting for me. What a delightful surprise! However, the your words left in me something far greater and more moving than delight.

For me, there is nothing more beautiful than meeting on the path of life a human being who carries within himself the soul of a poet. And I have discovered this poet in you as you read your poems to me that brightly lit London evening. Here is your letter carrying a poetic pulse to further enhance the picture and put me in a poetic mood. This was a true poem, and I am not saying this to patronize you. The proof is that it motivated me to compose a poem.

Saturday is a holiday in Israel, and it is a day on which Israelis flock to our occupied country and roam the streets under the protection of the occupation army. Hence, my feeling of alienation in my homeland further deepens.

When I began to compose my poem, I believed I would recall more memories of the distant past, the days of patience, poetry, and love; but what involuntarily happened was that the whole issue changed into what became my poem.

> It is out of my control, O Sami.
> I am possessed by the occupation.
> It is fixed idea, and there is nowhere to run to from it.
> So where can I run and how can I escape?

Do not force yourself to compose a poem in return, for I know that your concerns and job invade a poet's time and his/her poetic mood. All I hope is for you to accept my poetic gift and react to it emotionally. That will be more than sufficient for me.

It is perhaps funny for me to mention that I was invited a week ago to take part in a cultural evening and recite some of my poetry. I decided to read the letter I sent to you, but I had to make some additions or deletions to give the poem a more serious tone. Here I am sending you the poem in both old and new forms.

Please do not be embarrassed by my determination to fulfill my promise to stay in touch concerning Nimr Al-Udwan's poems, for when I do such things, I do them with such spontaneity and joy. Nothing makes me happier than doing things for others, let alone friends, and in spite of the short time that I have known you, I feel like I have known you for many years. I appreciate your kindness and familiarity, for it is my nature to like friendly people. In fact, I tend to like them at first sight. On the other hand, I tend to dislike some people at first sight without any justification or reason, other than my feeling that their soul lacks warmth and the beautiful emotional richness of self.

I hope you enjoyed your vacation in the land of beauty and art, and I wish you would visit us in the West Bank on your next break. I am ready to obtain a permit for you to visit, hoping this would give you the opportunity to become acquainted with our country and our situation. You're welcome to bring your Italian girlfriend, if you like; maybe she wishes to see her former husband's country. In any case, if you accept my idea, I am ready to work on turning it into a reality. You have only to inform me of your intent to visit the West Bank ahead of time and then send the date and time of your visit.

Do not force yourself to respond quickly to my letter. I am lazy about writing, and it could take me weeks before responding to my friends' letters. So, take your time. It's okay.

Sending you the most heartfelt feelings of friendship. God bless you.

Yours truly,
Fadwa Tuqan

6. I Wonder if My Poem Shook the Palm Tree?

"I will continue to summon my optimism. I am certain that I will not live long enough to take part in my struggling people's victory, for it is a long road ahead, and getting there will take two or three generations."

Nablus, November 3, 1975

Dearest Sami,

Blessed is that life that created you. The day before yesterday, following three weeks in Amman, I returned to my city to feel your two letters embrace me with open arms. The second letter arrived on the very same day I arrived. My soul found peace in the warm flow of your feelings, and I told myself I would respond tomorrow or after tomorrow after collecting myself.

I say blessed is that life that created you. Your two letters, or rather, you yourself came through the letters to touch my tired soul and to distract me, even for a little while, from this dizziness that engulfs me privately and publicly. In my private life, these days of oppression and usurpation have left me less relevant, for no one these days can remain oblivious to what is happening around him or her, both inside or outside. It is our destiny to be the generation of torture, steadfastness, and commotion. We did not come to this world a generation ago to enjoy the bliss of ignorance, and we did not come into the world later to enjoy a better tomorrow and a more beautiful world. As long as we are doomed to live this life, there is no escape from the burden.

The persisting and perplexing question is this: Can Israel inflict greater harm on us than that which we have already caused ourselves?

I am shocked by what is happening, trying to understand it all, only to become exhausted in vain. Those who conspire against us in the dark push us down, cutting off the ascent that we had started after October 1973. I am frightened, and I try to summon optimism, to no avail. There is inevitability in human nature, and pessimism is in my nature. When I go against the grain, I discover that my efforts are doomed, and I fail. Endless conspiracies constantly drain the strength of our Arab nation, but, in spite of it all, I maintain that the will to live is strong. Otherwise, why continue to struggle between the forces of darkness and the forces of a people who refuse to surrender?

I will summon my optimism. Surely, I will not live long enough to enjoy the victory of my struggling people, for it is a long road and getting there could take two generations or three. Let us work and be hopeful. What you said in your first letter about awakening from the long distracting road filled me with beauty and grandeur. You made me feel like the Virgin Mary when Gabriel whispered to her, "And take refuge under the palm tree and a generous number of dates will fall down." Have I shaken the palm tree with my poem? You are a true Arab palm tree, and the nation is more deserving of its dates.

Your talk of floating water plants with no roots did not surprise me. You who live in the heart of the declining European civilization cannot escape the sense of loss and regret. The feeling that you talked about I felt in the heart of every Arab I met there, and it made me happy. I was very pleased to discover this truth by myself and witness it with my own eyes. His truth confirmed another truth, that an Arab could never lose his or her roots, no matter how long the absence from the homeland and its people, for these roots remain firmly planted in each one forever and ever. The sense of belonging cannot be uprooted in the diaspora, even if you had thought that you did. The homeland lives in each one of you no matter where you are; you carry it in your hearts and eyes and in your travel bags and passports, even if they're not Arab. The nationality on the passport changes, but when it comes to the Arab face affixed inside it, who can change its beautiful original features, the features of sun and palm trees? It is impossible.

The promise you made to yourself makes me love you even more. And here I am cautioning myself. I have lost the talent for love many years ago. I see you laughing, and it makes me happy. I have two remaining talents: poetry and a burning passion for the land.

You asked me what I am doing these days. I am preparing a lecture about Palestinian poetry that I will present at the Youth Forum in Umm Al-Fahm, a small town in Israel, with its fertile land expropriated by Israel, leaving only the rocky mountain to its people. The youths there have no clear idea about the poets of Palestine and their poetry before 1948 because their situation cut them off from

Arab thought. They chose the topic of my lecture and asked me to conclude the seminar by reading some of my poetry.

As I told you in a previous letter, you are not obligated to respond quickly. Take your time to write whenever you feel like it. I love to give my friend some leeway and do not wish to burden him with my friendship.

I returned from Amman yesterday to learn that Qusay had asked about me. I was delighted with to visit with him and his wife. I do not know why I felt your presence; beautiful thoughts of you passed through my mind all evening.

You should have sung that song. I sometimes tell myself, “Maybe my taste in music is still backward and uncivilized. I admit that I love music and chanting Andalusian folklore music, but I don’t do myself injustice if I tell you that I don’t like western music. If I am unable to enjoy it and process it mentally, that does not mean I am incapable of appreciating it poetically. They sometimes make me cry and even exhaust me to some extent. My ears hear the soft tunes of Tchaikovsky’s Sixth Symphony making their way from the record player in a corner in the room next to me.

Fadwa

7. Consolation of the Spring

*"My soul yearns for absolute solitude and to preoccupation with reading the books that I love.
I am besieged by people and uncertain situations to the point of suffocation."*

Sami

I miss you.

I found this chapter about Bedouin poetry in an Arab-Israeli magazine. It appears that reconciling with the self is possible only at the moment of death; for as long as we are living, there is no way for us to escape the eternal struggle with the self. We cannot feel this shackle if we voluntarily follow those who are leading us. If we start to resist and try to walk away, all the pain will disappear.

O what lightning bolt has struck the woods of self, setting it on fire.

And O what suffering a torn and scattered soul feels. The political reality around us has killed in us our most beautiful and dearest possessions. It has killed harmony and agreement, the most fundamental components of psychological and spiritual wellbeing.

Literature, art, poetry, and music: for me, these arts represent the spring of richness and happiness that fuels my soul that cannot extend itself fully unless these fundamental things are present. Where is this spring? Where is it today? It has been sunk in the midst of political concerns and thoughts.

In short, politics became the bread, water, and bad air that we all breathe here. What bad times! When will our soul regain its spring? When?

I made some changes to the last poem about Jericho. After I compose a poem, I usually set it aside before reviewing it later with a different perspective and making some changes here and there. That was the poem after the new edits, along with a second poem I wrote immediately after sending the first.

Do you like these poems? Be candid and do not patronize me.

My soul yearns for absolute solitude and to spend my time reading the books that I love. I am besieged by people and uncertain situations to the point of suffocation. I want to go a distant, faraway place, to a place where no one knows me. I must travel this summer.

Do you plan to visit Jordan this year and when? Please let know if you wish to visit, so I can see you in Amman.

Once again, I miss you, I miss you a great deal.

Fadwa

8. Our Ability to Love!

"Life has taught me that all things come to full completion, that they come to fruition to wilt and wither away. This knowledge has made my soul more mature to the point that it has risen above all earthly desires, and I do not want anything for myself from this person."

Nablus, January 1, 1976

Dearest Sami,

Look, it's the first word I write and the first person I talk to on the morning of this new day. Happy New Year to you with a heart filled with joy, love, optimism, and hope.

In your last letter, you declared your hunger for my words, and you asked, Are there more? Are there more? You asked why I was being stingy, you talk about your thirst, and you ask me not to leave you standing so perplexed with your luggage outside a closed door. And you tell me, Give us love!

I will not leave perplexed, O dear one. Did you receive my gift dated December 12? Your eyes have grown attached to my clouds, and I hope that they have rained on you sufficiently to quench your thirst.

I don't know why writing to you takes so much effort from me. No, I rather do know why. I am not pleased with myself these days. Damn me, my road is lonely, and my friendship is miserable. I sometimes wonder: Why do we impose our misery on those we hold dear? Wouldn't it be better to talk to our loved ones just about things beautiful and joyful? So if we have nothing happy and beautiful to share, we had better keep quiet so as not to overburden each other with our misery.

By the way, a female friend from my childhood visited yesterday. I enjoy her friendship for her sincere conversations. Everything she says reflects real and true feelings. She had an amazing passion for life until the June war, and I used to get tired of her passion sometimes and scold her, Why are you eternally preoccupied with love? Isn't there enough pain and suffering in life to divert your attention away from love?

She would respond to me with spontaneity and sincerity, Trust me, if there's only one cedar tree left in the desert, I would have fallen in love with this cedar tree. Remember my friend, we can summarize the glory of humanity with one statement – the ability to love!

Her response used to leave me confused. Should I be happy, or should I feel sorry for her? Her theory in life was and still is giving, and her happiness lies in giving rather than taking. Her love targets only the lost, thirsty, or hungry. On the other hand, the love she gave to others was so motherly in an overwhelming way, and her love now resembles a mother's spontaneous love, flowing like sweet rivers and growing like flowers and trees according to the laws of nature. Her giving always reminds me of the fields of wheat.

In recent weeks, she has looked concerned and worried. I felt that she was holding something back, and she would not let it out. One day, I asked her, "What is wrong?"

She responded in a soft voice, "I'm in difficult emotional position." Then she proceeded to ask who wrote the following verse:

> I stood before the mirror and asked it
> And my eyelids denied everything they spotted
> I asked where the person is who stood here in the past
> When did she leave this place, O when
> The mirror ignored me and said without uttering a word
>
> That was then and this is the person that came after that!

I responded, "The poet is Ibn Zahr."

She said, "That is the tragedy, the damage that time has wreaked on a human being. What's more tragic is that a human being withers away, and the heart remains as passionate as ever."

It became apparent what she was hiding, and I came to know why she was feeling so confused. I told her, "Now I know. How did that happen?"

She then told me the story, about how it all started with little things that could happen to anyone any day without a sound, things that do not mean much, such as when he suddenly exited the elevator nimbly to welcome her and accompany her to his workplace.

She said, "At that moment, I felt something shining brightly inside of me, as though someone had flipped a switch, allowing the light to spread so brightly in me. The light shone brightly for a moment and then dimmed away when meeting, talking, and working with others. He insisted on taking a picture of us together to be published in the foundation's magazine. I do not like having my picture taken, for I don't like how it turns out. I resisted, but someone took a photograph of us. I suggested that I would give him a better photograph for publication if this one did not turn out well. I looked in my purse, found the picture, and handed it to him, but his hands were full of papers.

"He turned his left side to me and said, 'Put it in my pocket.'

"As I did that, a strange feeling came over me, as though he was closer to me than my own jugular vein. I felt awash with endless affection. As we left the foundation, he presented me with a perfume bottle. I said to myself, 'How strange. How did he know that I love this particular perfume?' Once we got into the car, and before he placed his hands on the wheel, he gave me a book, a collection Tchaikovsky's works, and said, 'I'm interested in drama these days."

"I have seen only The Seagull by Tchaikovsky and had read some of his short stories, and here I am going back to this collection of his works periodically to relive a world that this man who is dear to my life had lived before me.

"With all these little things, a strange seed fell into the grooves of my heart that I overlooked and ignored in the beginning. But it seems little, little things govern us, over which we have no control. After I returned home and received your first letter, that seed began to slowly grow into a giant tree bursting with passion and vision. I found myself drawing a new image of legendary young men with each new letter I received from these men, but I continued to feel the futility of it all. I did not understand what it meant. I felt unhappy with myself and needed to find a way out of all this siege."

I told her, "I agree that your situation is difficult, and that is a cause for concern and tension, but I have an idea. Why don't you adopt this person? Why don't you love him as a mother would? I am aware of these excessive motherly feelings that you have in your heart and soul."

She asserted that her feelings for him are equal to the love of all mothers on Earth combined, including those who had not yet given birth and those who have yet to be born. She also stressed that her soul had reached such maturity that it has allowed her to liberate herself from all material shackles.

Then she added, "Life has taught me that all things come to a full completion, to fruition in order to wilt and wither away. This knowledge has made my soul more mature to the point that it transcends all earthly desires, and I do not want anything for myself from this person. He renewed my life with zest that had been submerged in mud until everything beautiful and good had suffocated."

I just narrated to you the story of my friend. I found it be somewhat entertaining, despite the gloom that runs through it.

I still hold poetic evenings in various cities of the West Bank, and my last one was in the City of Hebron. After it ended and I went to the bedroom assigned to me, I noticed that there was no radio there. I told my host that I usually wake up early, regardless how late I stay up and that I like to listen to the early morning news. So she bought a radio. I was expecting to hear you in the morning, and the sound of your voice bloomed in my heart in that place where I never expected to meet you.

Fadwa

9. The Divine Palm Tree

"Some Fridays, I go to Jericho and live with the most beautiful trees God has ever created. There, palm trees are in abundance ..."

Nablus, February 24, 1976

Sami,

I wrote several letters to you and then tore them up time and time again.

I am unable to write. Maybe I will do that in a moment of self-reconciliation.

My girlfriend, as it seems, has turned into a Chekhov character. Inside, she is teaming with convoluted, conflicted emotions that make it hard for me to understand her.

I look at her and see a drama of tears mixed with the glow of laughter, but it is "laughter that resembles crying." She appears to be quiet and subdued, but no one is aware of the drama that runs just beneath the surface.

If I had accused you of having an estranged personality, what should I accuse myself of being? Falling back on imagination seems to be totally justified.

My friend recalls fabricated images, she imagines something that does not exist, and through this detachment from the outside world, she invigorates her imagination and emotional reactions and writes poetry.

Some Fridays, I go to Jericho and live with the most beautiful trees God has ever created. There, palm trees are in abundance.

Look, how great this tree is!

I am not aware of any other tree that carries so many beautiful meanings like this divine palm tree does.

Fadwa

There is no point in saying anything. In any case, may God forgive you! And thanks for your postcard from Italy, dated July 2.

10. Collecting the Pieces

"Hence, when you talk, something new is born …"

Nablus, April 26, 1976

Dearest Sami,

Your nostalgic feelings that I gathered from your letter transported me to a world of brightness and light as the borders of my loneliness began to recede, the ice of the world began to melt, and the scattered shrapnel of my life began to meld again. Hence, when you talk, something new is born ...

Thank you for remembering me in the two springs spread around you. As for me, wherever I land, your shadow drowns me in an eternal spring.

To avoid burdening you with this letter, I am choosing to sum it up quickly as I recall the saying: Do not overburden your loved ones, for in doing so, you may be boring them." That despite the fact that I really feel like talking to you tonight, and sleep has nothing but escape so far away.

I wonder if I will hear your voice tomorrow morning. Have a good evening, and now I will return to a book I have been reading for the last two days: *The Palestinian Question and Political Solution Projects.*

Fadwa

11. The Magic of Letters

"... for nothing can match their horror and grandeur, as they seep into hearts lovingly and rock us with tenderness, rebuilding the collapsing world inside us.
It is the amazingly creative power that can reassemble the splinters of a broken world."

Moving to the other world was not as easy as I had thought, for I could not do it, and I tried to maintain my self-control. I closed the *Palestinian Question* book and went to the kitchen to prepare a cup of coffee. I drink coffee in the middle of the night, just like any other time of the day. So here I am, returning to you with my coffee. You will have to put up with me, for my appetite for talking to you has overpowered me. How few are those who whet my appetite for conversation? It is my nature to keep quiet and listen. Often, I cannot motivate to engage in conversation.

And now, what do I want to say? I loiter in the hallways of museums and lecture halls and Oriental music halls, but I do it through your *This Morning* show.

You wrote on the postcard about the famous lantern artifact: "We were great; indeed, we were, and I hope we stop being Kantians and can overcome the past into a present and future teeming with rich civilizational contributions, just like that our forefathers presented to the world in foregone centuries."

How unfortunate it is that the grandchildren of those innovative creators of that great art now find themselves mired in the darkness of poverty, ignorance, and disease. All the while the classes that exploited religion out of selfishness now control the fate of miserable Muslim nations and their resources. For that reason, I am against religion, especially when it turns into a vehicle for exploitation in serving a specific class of people when it can be nothing more than the first and foremost enemy of the people. Given my own personal inclinations and strong determination to protect my personal freedom and independence, I sometimes wish that communism would sweep all Arab oil-producing countries.

On that same beautiful postcard, you quoted Ibn Arabi: "Now letters are a nation." I am never ceased to be amazed at the magic of letters and the power they carry. However, as much as I am amazed and impressed, I am also filled with terror and fear, especially when, in the hands of villains, they become black magic by distributing false accusations and false rumors. At that point, I feel that a demon has possessed the ominous letters, making me feel sick to my stomach. The circle of my disgust widens to engulf the human creator of the letter, for humans are the only creatures capable of fabricating lies and injecting deadly poison through letters.

But I then go back to the dear letters, asking for their forgiveness and extolling their glory. Nothing can match their horror and grandeur, as they seep into hearts lovingly and caress us with tenderness, rebuilding the collapsing world inside us. It is the amazingly creative power that can reassemble the splinters of a broken world.

One other thing, dear Sami, that causes me to contemplate: Can these letters convey the truth of our feelings? Can you sense a strong emotion when you read my writing:

"I have loved so and so; he stands in the river of my life as a huge barrier obstructing its flow." It is impossible.

Once when I asked you to recite an Andalusian poem sung by Fairuz, "Why is the mullah waking up from his drunkenness," you did not know that you fulfilled a desire to answer a question that you had said was impossible to answer. You told me at the time that this poem cannot be found in the music library. However, to my surprise, you presented the poem a few weeks ago on your show, and after the interview with Ibrahim Al-Areed Al-Bahraini ended, the choir chanted, "Will our days in the Gulf return?" I was very happy to hear it. I had been turning the dial at that time, and the recordings were restricted to your chats. In any case, before I owned this radio, the things you said disappeared into thin air with the radio waves. I lost them, and I could not return to your words and recall the joy I felt hearing your voice. But now, I feel you are a hostage of a number of these tapes.

Talking about stream of consciousness and memories, I have the Chekhov collection lying on the edge of the table, and I listen to them when I cannot fall asleep. I dive into the world of Chekhov teaming with internal human complexities, like a collection of epic poetry.

I find myself drawn to the play, *Uncle Vania*, more than anything else composed by this great man. I am drawn to the pain that oozes from every direction of the play. Perhaps pain was the only hero in this play, for when Sonia, who is no less miserable than her uncle is, rests her head on his shoulder to ease his pain, I feel the harshness of life summarized in the few sentences Sonia utters:

"Poor Uncle Vania, you are crying. You've never known joy, but wait, in the end, we will all rest!"

Thus, by the time death becomes the only peace for human beings, misery would have reached its ultimate peak. The poet Al-Mutannabi said something similar: "The ultimate disease is for you to believe that death is a cure."

What drew my attention in the author's introduction is when she says that Chekhov's biographers are baffled by the conflict and contradiction between his sense of humor and lightheartedness and passion for life. His plays and short stories, in spite of the humor they contain, leave a sad impression as a result of unfulfilled passions, sense of frustration, and absolute misery.

In my opinion, this contradiction is justifiable, for Chekhov was a modest, humble, pure soul, and the shyer a person is, the more he or she would wears a mask of laughter and joy to conceal the hidden secrets of a tortured soul. I say this from experience, for I myself, given my extremely sensitive and shy nature, put on a mask of cynicism and laughter with my friends to shield me from the harsh curiosity that penetrates the depth of my soul. My brother Nimer was also like that. He was merry with a bossy personality that prompted laughter and humor everywhere he went, and nobody knew that he was a lonely, sad man.

Some say the most depressed nations are those most capable of singing, and perhaps this supports what I am trying to say in this regard.

Good night, and I hope to see you tomorrow morning. How unfortunate I would be if I heard that artificial fake voice! If that happens, I will turn off the radio immediately, for I cannot pretend. (Of course, this is just between us, not for publication or sharing with others). There is no need to hurt other people's feelings without justification.

Fadwa

12. Hoping to See You …

*"I repeat my plea to keep the visit a secret,
for my strength and mood do not serve me right
when it comes to social duties."*

Nablus, May 2, 1976

Dearest Sami

I will be in England on July 1 for four days, and I have reserved a place to stay in through a travel agency.

If I am lucky and you are not yet on leave, I will call you that day in the evening. I prefer to call your home number (at 2721000) that you wrote down for me last year.

(This is not to be talked about to anybody!)

I had told my friend Dr. Fu'ad about the unconfirmed possibility that I would visit, but I will see him in any case at the end of the day.

I repeat my plea to keep the visit a secret, for my strength and mood do not serve me right when it comes to social duties toward my relatives there, and how many they are! It is enough for me to see you.

Fadwa

13. Alone with the Days

"I have lived my entire life alone in misery and pain without anyone near or far sharing any of my concerns. But what shall I do with this soul tortured by the misery of others?"

Nablus, August 6, 1976

Dearest Sami,

I kept thinking all day today – Friday – about writing to you. Maybe this letter comes a little late, as I was supposed to write to you upon my return, but when I came back, I found – as usual – many concerns awaited me, including the arrest of my niece in Nablus. Here we are awaiting the results of the investigation, and even though we are certain she is innocent, we remain very concerned because of her deteriorating health. She is anemic with kidney pain, and her mother – my sister – had a stroke. Any psychological tension affects her gravely.

I sometimes wonder: Why do I have to carry other people's worries? Does anyone feel for me? I have lived my entire life suffering alone, worrying alone, and crying alone without anyone near or far sharing my concerns. But what do I do with this soul eternally tortured by the misery of other people? There's nothing I can do about it.

Would you believe that my belongings are still scattered all over the place? My clothes, books, and papers, and this chaos around me lies shriveled next to the emotional mess inside me. This will be the subject of a long discussion apart from this letter. My problem is that I pose too many questions to myself, and I even sometimes posit them in different ways to make it even more complicated and strange, further confusing myself, and the question remains banging and banging in my head without a satisfactory answer.

In any case, here I am coming back to a world that is different from the world of last month, a world that carries not a touch of beauty or dreaming. It is sad that a dream cannot be relived, cannot repeat

itself, and yet the ugliness of the waking hours is repeated on a daily basis, and we live and relive them again and again.
I wrote to Mr. Amen Abdel Hafiz upon my arrival in Nablus and asked him about the possibility of postponing the broadcast of the recording until the beginning of October.

Concerning the word (Bate') stamina, I remember that we wondered if the linguistic root of this word is from the Fuscia language. I checked it in the dictionary and found this explanation: "Bata'a Bat'an: his neck or joints became elongated, and he is abta' and she is bat'aa, and Al-Abt'a is the chubby person."

Therefore, the colloquial use of this word is not from its official definition in Fuscia, and it means strength or power. So when we say, I don't have any stamina (bate'), we are simply saying we lack strength or stamina.

I arrived in Nablus at noon on Monday, and I stayed in Amman for one day on Sunday. I left the Parker pen set at my sister's in Amman, for there is a prohibition from bringing ink pens across the bridge into the West Bank. I will still get the set from my cousin when he arrives at the airport. Lod Airport travelers have permission to bring their pens into the West Bank. Rest assured, I will not abandon a gift you have given to me, no matter what.

Lots of love
Fadwa

14. Write to Me

"The truth and nothing but the truth is all I ask."

Jerusalem, November 17, 1976

Dearest Sami,

What's happening? Write me about the reasons for your absence.

Something in the air is making me uncomfortable. It seems that the story has turned into a "scandal!"

Please write candidly and please be clear.

The truth and nothing but the truth is all I ask.

Write me before you go to bed tonight. Please!

Please do write!

15. Absence…Absence…

"I wonder when will I hear your voice again?
I hope you are well, in any case."

Sami…

Absence…Absence…Absence! You're not on "This Morning", nor on "The World This Noon", nor "Around the Arab World", or the "The World This Evening."[8] Where are you then? Are you sick with the flu now spreading all over the UK, or what?

I am worried sick for you. I am praying for your recovery, if you are ill, and I feel so lonely because of your absence.

For two weeks now, we are under collective punishment due to the closure of the bridge, and we are all prohibited from leaving for Amman; otherwise, I would have gone to Amman to send a telegram to inquire about you.

I do not like to send telegrams from here that might draw people's attention. Some post office employees are overly curious.

I wonder when I will hear your voice again? In any case, I hope you are well.

I have no other concern these days but to know that you are well.

Fadwa

8 These are the titles of programs that Sami presented on the BBC World Service.

16. Confusion

"O how confused I am by your long absence . . ."

November 19, 1976

Dearest Sami,

Here you are coming back to me again, and I now feel relieved. Yesterday – Thursday – I spotted you on “The World This Noon”, and this morning – Friday – I saw you with the beauties of the world, so I prayed in gratitude to the creator of beauty.

O how much your long absence has confused me, and how afraid I was that you were involved in a problem at work because of me.

May this new year – and every new year – bring you blessings, love, and beauty, and may all your days be a festival of poetry and emotions.

Fadwa

17. Love and Eternity

"It is true that my feelings for you feel eternal, but they sometimes intensify in an authoritarian and controlling way."

Nablus, December 9, 1976

Dearest Sami,

Here I am sitting with you on this quiet morning covered with clouds. Before I say anything else, I beseech you – for my part – to delete from our dear Jubilee dictionary the word "rocks," for this word and all its aggressive and offensive connotations can have no place among us, for there is nothing between us that necessitates an exchange of rock throwing. And please forget the incident of "May God greet the Arab brother", for that miserable incident will remain an isolated event in the book of our friendship and love for each other, and will not have a sister or sisters like it.

The reason why I asked the question that you misinterpreted is my concern for you because you had stopped presenting your usual shows for me that were worth "One thousand years what you (humans) count": a Qur'anic verse" that reminds me of the "theory of relativity." What made me even more concerned was the delay in the broadcasting my recordings later than the approximate time you had given me. This forced me to assume that you may have had a problem with the BBC because of me. Maybe the words I penned to you later on in the postcards and through the handsome Bedouin explained the reason why I was asking about your absence and silence that confused me. As for the "scandalous" statement, I have deleted it – as you have asked me to do – from our dictionary (that we created in the Jubilee of our jasmine, daisies, and poppies), and how much emotional insinuation was there is in your statement. I am not sure about what the poppy flower is. I believe we call it "habaq (basil)" in Palestine, but I will double-check in Amman and ask about this flower.

As for the correspondence and in-kind treatment, please trust that the heart of your loving friend always casts aside all math equations in any of its dealings with loved ones. Those who love, O dear Sami, do not send invoices to their loved ones. For people who love each other, there is nothing as such as a debtor and a creditor. I told you once, and I will repeat it again that I would be seriously upset if I learned that you were forcing yourself to carry an additional burden because of me. If I begged you in my letter, which you likened to a postcard, to respond quickly, that was because I was very worried about you.

When I sat down at the table this morning with pen and paper to respond to your letter, I began to feel the birth of a new poem in me, and as usual in such a case, I froze in my chair, completely motionless and began to daydream. O, if you would see your friend in one of her poetic trances, you would have recalled seeing an Indian monk in contemplative meditation. In any case, the poem was completed by 1:30 in the afternoon, and I wished that it would find its way to you at the same moment to carry inner calm and peace to you, because I felt you were upset when you wrote your letter.

Mail between Mount of Jarzeem and St. John Road takes twelve days. What a long mail road! Four of the twelve days can be saved if the letter is dropped in a post office box in Jerusalem; mail in the West Bank, in contrast to Jerusalem, goes through two stages, given the odd administrative situation under occupation there, which delays incoming and outgoing mail to and from the West Bank. Out of my keenness to get the letter to you as soon as possible, I took the letter – the poem to be exact – and traveled to Jerusalem to deposit it in a mailbox at a post office there. Thus, I made sure it would get to you sooner than usual. I hope you received it and that you liked it, just like I did. (As usual, I might make some changes to it.)

On your *This Morning Show* today – Thursday, December 19 – I felt you so deeply. It is true that my feelings for you seem eternal, but they sometimes intensify in an authoritarian and controlling way.

Maybe the music or the song that you presented on the show had something to do with that, for music is like magic to me. A beautiful song has a strange and exciting impact on me:

> All of life could be insignificant save for one hour
> and earth might be insignificant save for one location

When the melodious voice of Abdel Wahab started to flow – and how much I love this magnificent voice – immediately after I had finished talking about stored memories without any break, I discovered a new taste for this song, as though I had not heard tens of times in my life. The song carried me to Jubilee where I drowned in a July dream, and pictures and pictures started playing in my head. There was one particular picture, rather a nicely shaped silhouette of a human being standing in the fuzziness of a room with closed drapes, except for one narrow opening from which a very thin stream of light is flowing. A silhouette from a mysterious world other than the real world, standing in a particular place and in a particular way in a dark room. This unreal scene sticks in my memory, my eyes, and my senses and imposes itself with force and determination.

Sami: This is a special request. Please pass by Jubilee in Chelsey and tell that particular place: "Greetings to you, O that place consecrated by pure love."

Thanks for your efforts and concern to broadcast my radio recordings. The most beautiful thing about your morning show in its new format is your fixed presence on it every day. I hope it will last for a very long time!

I was so happy when you said that I am with you at work and at home. You won't believe how happy I am to know that you said you hug my letters every night. (My friend) that I introduced you to commented, I wish I could replace them!

I am tortured by your longing for me. I wish the bridges extended by this longing would bring you to me in the flesh, for your eternal spiritual presence in my heart is no longer enough for me. I miss you, and I yearn to see you in an unimaginable way.

Have you seen the play *Ivanov* now being played by Shakespeare Troupe in London? The theater is near the BBC building, and I would imagine you will not waste any opportunity to spend an evening with our dear Chekhov. Did anyone go with you to see it? I wish I could be there with you!

It's Christmas and the New Year holiday season, and I wish you on this occasion and on every occasion a long life full of good health and love, of beauty and giving. With all my love.

Fadwa

18. Taming Solitude

"I do not know how I will face my daily life after your departure, but I know there is no escape for me from training myself to live in the arid desert that will swallow my coming days."

Nablus, January 4, 1977

Dearest Sami,

My rejoicing about your daily appearance was destined not to last. I miss you a great deal. I have grown apathetic about listening to the others, for listening to them only deepens my sense of loneliness, even though I am certain about your return to me once again. But how can I face it if you had left my mornings forever? I never expected you to make such a decision. I thought you were tied to your current work with the eternal bond of familiarity and routine until work at the radio became an instinct. As for me, I do not know how I will face my daily life after your departure. I do know there is no escape for me from training myself to live in the arid desert that will swallow up my coming days and that will be devoid of your morning presence and from your daily sweet and lively chats. Who will charge my faint days with light and warmth, if your voice is no longer there?

You tell me that your new work in Italy shortens the distance between us by one half, but I wonder when was long distance an obstacle between us? I am familiar with one road to you and that is the road to the heart, and how short this road is. Do not believe that I am being driven by selfishness, for the real motive behind what I am saying is loneliness and isolation, and I have already begun to feel them now.

Also, your statement in the last letter that (life here is unbearable) instilled misery in my heart, because it tells me you are not happy with your present situation. I don't know if you are unhappy with the nature of your work or because of the economic crisis strangulating the whole world. Your word "here" did not specify the location that has become a source of unhappiness to you and that made you feel dismayed and unhappy about your environment. In any case, I hope that the Almighty will bring you relief after difficulty and bless each and every step you take whenever you are and wherever you go.

Perhaps the flu that you fought off for a very long time was the reason for your inability to tolerate your current situation. Damn be this flu that leaves and for many months leaves worse effects on the nerves, making patients irritable, tense, and angry.

In any case, I will keep your search for a new job a secret. In the meantime, I will continue to wait for your morning visits on the radio and will see where you will end up.

For the first, you start your letter with poetry. And with "Each day, my love, I wait for the mail, etc. I want to write to you every day, was not for that "complex" I told you about in a previous letter. I wish you would know how hard I try to control my feelings. I wish you would know how hard it is to withhold the rain pouring from my heart and soul, and how, how many times it occurred to me to stop exchanging letters with you. More than once, I wrote a letter that I did not send. My intention is to stop sending letters, but before I do that, I want to start to feel the ice of loneliness and a form of suffocation, just for merely thinking that that balcony is closed without us. This is the balcony you referred to in your poetic lines as the "balcony of the heart to the heart." The closure of that balcony means cutting off sunlight and air from me.

Speaking about the poetry lines you started your letter with, I am still waiting for your poem to fulfill your desire with utmost pleasure. I see you are fully absorbed in poetry, and I have recorded all the poems that you have read over the last few months, the last of which was "The Birth." It was obvious that you had a cold as you read them. (Don't be upset, the coarseness in your voice as a result of the cold is cute and sweet.)

This is the first letter I write you in the new year, and I don't know if you are back in England or still in Italy. Will this letter wait for you or will you wait for it? Greetings to you in both cases, and greetings to Jubilee and St. John and all mailmen.

Fadwa

19. Door Number 14…Who Will Open It?

"Suddenly, a sealed wound reopens … all the beautiful things are in pain … I force myself not to remember … that takes a lot of effort from me … the sudden psychological change shocks the self… leaving a crack in the beautiful sensation."

Dearest Sami,

July departed, leaving in the memory a package of golden rays with brightness cannot be dimmed. Here is the heart taking refuge under the stillness of the night. A memory runs through, shedding light on the secrets of the depths. Secrets come to the fore; the tape of colored pictured runs through…streets…cars…red buses… gardens…a door, carrying the number 14 opens and closes to pens and papers scattered all over a small white round table…a small old transistor radio. Bach or Handel…Mozart or Wagner…a head peeps in to listen closely. A small shrub climbs up the wall of a garden, vines that have yet to ripen. A burger meal in an American restaurant. Cambridge theater on Earlham Street and an unforgettable evening with Chekhov… the plight of the three sisters tortured by the boring life in the village, eager to live life in Moscow in its deeper meaning, taking me back to the time of my own plight in ancient prison that assassinated two-thirds of my life. A new car rushes me like fleeting time, giving me generously one hand and taking it back with cruel sadism. Yellow and green traffic lights forcing it to pause for a second or two, at which time stops and then it starts racing again. July has a green hand that strokes the body, changing the cycle of seasons and the law of nature. The world of the impossible, impossible to the extent that memory itself starts screaming before it. Impossible for all this to be a real world; it is an epic world, O July. It has all the strangeness of a dream and all the seriousness of a dream.

Suddenly, a sealed wound reopens…all the beautiful things are in pain…I force myself not to remember…that takes a lot of effort from me…the sudden psychological change shocks the self…leaving a crack in the beautiful sensation. This feeling was at its fullest a moment ago, just a moment ago. Why do beautiful things feel this pain? Why is the face of the world being distorted?

(And you may hate something when it is good for you). Hence, there had to be a third person…there had to be a Yahoo to end it all and for a more beautiful, grander and richer thing to come about. With the emergence of a third person, the death sentence against the new thing that has risen and grown over the last continuous months is adjourned. That beautiful thing that had lost its value in my feelings and self; the dream story that turned in a second into a funny vaudeville … it was important for yahoo to emerge for it to restore its value and beautiful meaning. Thanks to the third person, for he has moved in me my hesitant and contemplative Hamiltonian nature, and had Atilla not had the cautious, suspicious personality, Yahoo's devilish plan would have not succeeded, and the tragedy would not have happened.

Therefore, wait and do not assassinate the "dream" before you discover the truth. Then, then what? Here I am saying with Rambo: "The world is good; I bless this life"… my emotions are overtaken with a symphony that life cannot play any better or greater than!

No doubt I burden you with my digressions. Let me stop at this and let me land with you to an inescapable (plain from reality), for all at once, the mail sent me the book *Publish It Not*, the tape of my sung poem, and the papers I had forwarded to myself from the Chelsea post office. I am overwhelmed by the feeling of gratitude and from the depth of myself, my loving self, I thank you.

I hope you enjoyed your trip to Europe. As for your promised trip to Nablus, it will remain to me a hopeless case. I have learned not to wait for anything, and I explain it to myself because of my fear of a harsh surprise. However, in the coming days and on the day that the winds will blow you into my city, then every single emotion in me will welcome you, and the Mounts of Ibal and Jerzeem will embrace you with the kindness of "a mother on a nursing baby."

The contents of your letter raised some astonishment in me, for my impression in our meetings says something different than what you stated in your letter. You did not seem to be one of those who are lonely or feel the void if a friend departs. However, I did receive your letter with kindness and love, and I have deposited it in a warm place in my heart and soul, even if they are just words.

(My niece is still under arrest.)

In the name of maintaining security, everything is justified. The native Indians were exterminated in order to maintain the security of America, and one million Algerians were killed to protect the security of the French occupation of Algeria, and more than one million Vietnamese were killed to protect the capitalist security of America, and so on and so forth. The public has usurped its security to maintain the security of the existing regimes that mutilate the face of the world! This poor face of the world, in light of the large number of mutilation cases. I feel inclined to become a Sufi hermit. I wish your nun sister would take me there.

I have composed another new poem about July, but I have yet to put the last touches on it. I wonder if there's anything new with respect to your colleague(s). Please let me know. I feel your absence every morning!

Fadwa

20. A Strange World

I deemed it best for us to meet and discuss this issue, then part without love or hate."

O Dear One,

I have learned that you have shared with some of your colleagues the secrets I have entrusted with you. There is an upset person whom I have rebuffed and who is vexed by my silence in the face of his pettiness. I am nearly certain that this person works in the darkness to sabotage our friendship in collusion with one other person or more.

My feelings for you are no longer as important to me as lifting the mask off the face of Yahoo who is lurking somewhere and to leave the cycle of ambiguity engulfing the atmosphere in a creepy manner.

For this reason, I deemed it best for us to meet and discuss this issue, then part without love or hate, in a healthy and proper way, for there is no reason for our innocent friendship to turn into a toxic enmity filled with hate and darkness.

Do not be a naïve child, and keep this letter a secret, so that the devils will not attempt other demonic acts. Beware of the evil of the frustrated friends around you, for a frustrated person is saddened by the happiness of a lucky friend, and this is a psychological truth that I believe.

May God greet our Arab brother!

We have learned that you have left, and we were not surprised!

And we learned that you did not leave, and we were not surprised!

We remembered a saying we heard just a few days ago from a philosopher who asked:

“Where is the truth?”

And he continued on his way and did not wait for the reply!

It is a strange world full of contradictions. As for the smart person, he or she is the one who drowns themselves with cool indifference and does not feel sad for anything nor happy for anything.

And whoever has led a life like mine would know, etc.

21. Under the Yoke of the Self

"There are many things I would like to talk to you about,
but I have a complex about writing letters,
and I have denied myself the opportunity to bare myself
on paper and in correspondence."

Nablus, October 20, 1977

Dearest Sami,

Why apologize? Any letter from you is valuable to me in its own self, be it written a rush or slowly. Please be assured that the subject of your proposal concerns me more than the joy your letter or a small card brings me. I will not forgive myself for its ugly selfishness, if I felt one day that I am burdening you with any obligation in addition to those dictated on you in your studies and work. So please go ahead, and may God bless your steps, and do not worry about anything other than fulfilling your beautiful ambition.

As for me, I truly regret having opened up to you about your departure and missing you, but since you asked, I will reply briefly. The truth is that I am not certain about anything anymore; rather, I am in permanent loss. Even at the height of my joy, I could not escape an inner bleeding that I always so keenly tried to hide so as not to spoil the moment. It's an emotional contradiction that continuously devours me – deep joy for the presence of *July* with me and stinging feeling about July's absence from me. Even my spontaneity in writing poetry became spoiled under the yoke of emotional duality and contradiction. I tried in my poem about July to reflect this emotional contradiction.

I am the one begging you to be excused now, especially after what you confirmed to me in your letter. There are many things I wish I could tell you, but I have a complex about writing letters, and I forbade myself from baring my soul on paper. However, if we were destined to meet again one day – and my heart is telling me we won't – then I will tell what I do not like to pen here. Otherwise, I will let darkness drop its curtains on this chapter forever.

I received yesterday with your letter the postcard you sent from Foligno, dated September 6. As for the last two postcards, they have not arrived yet. Regular mail takes longer; it can take up to two months or longer. It's okay. How beautiful it is for one to know that his loved ones carry them in their hearts and minds while traveling.

I listen to the emotional songs of my compatriot D. Walid, and perhaps my emotional outpourings will follow. I hope you will recite to me one morning a guitar tune by Julian Braille that combines the beauty of the East and the West. Some of your colleagues broadcast it two or three times before, and I could not record it.

I feel this sad gloom, and I miss you.

Fadwa
Nablus, October 25, 1977

22. Madea's Last Confession

"I was lost, Sami; lost in every sense of the word, and I could not find myself on that desert road that I was crossing alone in silence and confusion."

I did not know that my silence hurts you and makes you sad. Had I had the slightest knowledge about it, I would not have stopped writing to you at all. But I will punish myself for a mistake I did not even know I was committing, and the punishment I will exact on myself is to exceed all the limits I had promised myself by not baring my soul in letters.

Yes, in this letter, I will break all the limits, and I will be like the legendary (Madea) created by the Latin poet Ovid, who is known for her infamous statement: "I see the good and acknowledge it and commit the bad." However, the difference is that Madea used to engage in bad deeds to hurt others, but I bring harm only to myself. Yet, my confidence in you is great. May any malicious gossiper who betrayed what we had go to hell (and no one can spoil that).

All there is to this silence that I complained about to you is that I am not sure about anything anymore as I told you in my letter five days ago. I was lost, Sami, lost in every sense of the word, and I could not find myself on that desert road that I was crossing alone in silence and confusion.

I started to feel lost right after I left you that Saturday morning on July 21. I left you in your car without turning to look in your eyes before getting out of the car. I ran to the hotel to give you the freedom to take off and start the journey of loss. When I went back to my country, I decided not to overburden you with my letters and not to force you to respond to it out of a sincere desire to leave you in peace. But believe me when I stress that that silence did not separate me from you one single minute. Each and every cell in my body swims in your eternal presence, and my feeling that you are present exceeds all bounds.

I am certain now about what I mean to you, for your lines wreak of sincerity and loyalty. They put you in a firm place in my heart that no Yahoo can penetrate, and the scepter of doubt cannot penetrate its walls or shake its foundations.

I now know and am certain of this shared feeling between us, and your statement in the letter that contained a clip from the *New York Times* that (…What happened between us was not simply a casual thing; but rather the chisel that changed the course of your life and cannot go away…] confirms that. These beautiful words break all language molds in my hands, and when I attempt to pour my feelings into them, all words in such a case appear hollow, weak, and faint when faced with the true momentum and density of emotions. The language that my soul speaks remains drowned out of sight and in mystery to the point that it leaves me unable to express myself. O what influence did those words have on my heart. I cannot bear to see you in pain because of me, and here I am as you can see, killing the silence before your eyes so that you would be sure of my feelings.

Sincere thanks to you for reminding to send the review of the book *After the Guns are Silenced.* I had listened to the interview you held with Sayyed Ahmad, the author, and I recorded it. As a result of his conversation with you, I learned that the author made some additions to the English edition. I had read some synopses of the book published in Beirut in *Al-Quds* Arabic newspaper and I will read the *Times*' review as soon as I am done with this letter. Do not bother to buy the English edition of the book for me, for the book – any book – these days can be bought with British pounds, so it is not fair for you to pay that much. I say it sincerely and honestly.

In any case, our complicated political experience over these years have led me to believe that the ebb and flow in this region is endless, for all the introductions were that we now deem reasonable and acceptable as a base will soon become useless, as things are moving at an amazing speed. Our cause is intertwined with the interests of the two superpowers which negate each other's presence in this part of the world. How can one develop a clear political vision in an area that stands on shifting sands?

Did you receive my letter and the poem, *July*? I might make some changes to it, for I am not happy about some of its parts.

Lastly, my friend and companion, all my love to you. You, the eternal July.

Fadwa

Addendum About the Poem "A Symphony from London"

1. I consolidated the two verses
   "The bells of silence have set in, and the world disappeared
   The world disappeared in a moment of spectacular death."
   I added the last words to give it an ending. Thus, the segment "Jubilee Place" becomes the second segment, and the poem is now comprised of four segments, similar to how symphonies are composed.

2. For the first time, I listened to Fairuz: "They say love kills time." Don't you see that it carries the same tragic nature of my poem? I mean that inevitable ending or the curse of time that puts an end to everything. The song also reminded me of William Tell, or rather, the quote from this legendary hero: "Love makes time go fast and time can make love go slow."

3 Never mind the perfume bottle. Please keep it until whenever. I will visit my relative when she visits her city Nablus.

4. Do you intend to try the perfume Heretic or are you not a B.B. man?

23. Everything Comes to An End, Except Memories!

"The days have exhausted the meaning of things ... and bitterness has shrouded the present and future in its misery; there is nothing left except that happy past rife with colored memories ..."

December 28, 1977

Dearest Sami,

Thanks, from the bottom of my heart. I don't know what to say. Oftentimes, surprise stands in the way of us saying anything, especially when it has such a profound impact.

I was deeply saddened by the bleak ending of our beautiful friendship without justification or reason. Everything was in perfect harmony and mutual understanding. Then, without any introduction, life between us became motionless.

For my part, I was always keen on letting things flow without any complication. I even hid from you the hearsay and gossip about me by some of your friends. It was enough for me to justify their gossip on the grounds of ulterior motives that concerned you in the first place, more than me. I remember hinting slightly at these rumors, but you sent me a letter begging me to erase that "scandalous phrase" from the dictionary we planted at Jubilee with roses and poppies or wildflowers. I deleted the statement and refrained from discussing and responding, and this is my usual stand vis a vis such issues, for life is short and there is not enough time for testiness and hatred.

I never believed in eternal relationships, for everything comes to an end. And I could already see that the curse that puts an end to all beautiful things was destined to prevail. But I wanted an ending that was clear of impurities, the impurities of complications and bitterness. I wished for a gradual, natural ending that would leave us both in peace with ourselves, happy with the stored richness and wealth of the experience. But you opted for the difficult winding road, and it was an utterly futile road, devoid of any meaning for me. However, I managed to tame myself as I have become "acclimated" to the arid rocky land to which I was suddenly transported without any introduction, and I managed to give in to a despair that I found comfort in, and I was completely at peace.

It did not occur to me that you will come around again from America…the letter of your dear sister Thurayya arrived like Handel's music trumpet. It awoke me from my comfortable, healthy slumber and thrust me in the whirlwind of new passion!

I found myself writing about "Solutions and the Void" and the feelings of missing you that have come out of their hiding hole all of a sudden, even though I had stopped planting the poems of love in my notepad a long time ago.

With these lines is a poem that is six months old. It remained asleep between my papers ever since I carried it in my briefcase upon my return from holiday last summer. The poem found its way to the Jewish lieutenant's room on the bridge. He read it and then looked at me – kindly – and returned it silently. I left the room cursing these bad times and wondering bitterly: "Was man created so that he could fall into the trap of a world ruled by evil and wanton?" I did not find an answer to counter this statement.

Please do not ask to be excused and do not feel sorry for anything. Also, don't bother about coping.

The days have exhausted the meaning of things, and bitterness has shrouded the present and future in its misery. There is nothing left except that happy past, rife with colored memories: green, red, blue, etc.

I am delighted that you returned to find that you are still a friend and a lover who is always in the heart. Regardless of what happened and what will happen, I am delighted to talk to you, for I miss hearing you. There are prints from life that we cannot erase from our depth, and your prints will remain, remain forever. I am getting older, and everything may be destroyed, except for beautiful memories and dear prints.

Fadwa

24. Greetings from the Breeze of the "Thames"

Three years of silence and alienation
    And how beautiful it is to reconcile with loved ones
We have forgiven the guilt of time
    And how unjust has time been and how much it has transgressed
    **

Thurayya, O sister, o loved one
    For lovers have strange moods
How strange is their nature
    Strongly shaped by the violence of conflict
    **

They are sometimes in perplexing anxiety
    And sometimes it is their destiny to be in a state of contradiction
Their contradictions are destined
    With bad luck and good luck revolving around them

And their world remains full of visions and concerns
    And the truth may remain a dream
However, we are in love with love regardless
    Of the ebbs and flow of its tide

The breeze of Al-Salt freshens the air of Jubilee
    And the sun of "Nablus" shines eternally
And the garden of contentment is yearning in the shade
    With blooming roses and poppies

May the eyes of the gloaters never rest
    And may the disgraced never find peace
We shall remain in spite of the haters
    Overflowing with love and friendliness

Greetings from the breeze of the Thames
    And the yearning, O Thurayya, will remain unrequited

Here is Fadwa, and here is dear Sami
    They were pleased to meet each other, and rosy this meeting was

London, Summer 1980

Addendum

A sample of Fadwa's original handwritten letters and photographs with Sami Haddad in London

نابلس ٣/١١/١٩٧٥

العزيز الاثير سامي ،

مباركة هي الحياة التي خلقتك . اول امس ، وبعد غياب ثلاثة اسابيع في عمان، عدت الى مدينتي لتتلقاني رسالتاك بذراعين مفتوحتين . الرسالة الثانية وصلت يوم وصولي بالذات . استكانت روحي الى دفء مشاعرك المتدفقة، وقلت اكتب الرد غداً او بعد غد حيث اكون قد لملمت بعض الاجزاء من نفسي المبعثرة هنا وهناك .

اقول مباركة هي الحياة التي خلقتك واعيد القول ، فقد جاءتني الرسالتان او بالأصح جئتني انت من خلالهما لتمسح بيدك الدافئة على روحي المتعب، ولتشغلني ولو الى حين عن هذا الدوار الذي يلفني من الصعيدين، الخاص والعام . الخاص اصبح في هذه الايام ، ايام القهر والاستلاب ، اقل اهمية ، فلا احد يستطيع ان يبقى في هذا الزمن لامبالياً بما يجري حوله في الداخل او في الخارج . لقد كتب علينا ان نكون جيل العذاب والصلب والجلجلة ، لم نأت قبل هذا الزمن الرديء فننعم بالجهل ، ولم نتأخر قليلاً لننعم بالغد الافضل والعالم الاجمل . وما دام قد حُكم علينا بالحياة فلا مفر من حمل العبء.

السؤال الملح والمحير هو : هل تقدر اسرائيل ان توقع بنا اذى اكبر من هذا الذي نوقعه نحن بأنفسنا ؟ مشدوهة انا بما يجري ، ابحث عن معناه فأعيا واتعب عبثاً . المتآمرون علينا في الظلام يزلون بنا الى تحت ليقطعوا علينا طريقنا التصاعدي الذي بدأناه بعد اكتوبر ١٩٧٣ . اني خائفة ، استدعي التفاؤل ، اوحي به لنفسي ولكن عبثاً . هناك حتمية في الطبائع ، والتشاؤم هو الغالب على طبيعتي ، وانا حين احاول ان اتخذ موقفاً اقوى من طبيعتي ، أو to go against the grain كما يقولون عندكم ، يخيب مسعاي وافشل.

مؤامرات لانهائية لا تعمل دائبة على سحب عصب القوة من امتنا العربية. ولكني اظل اقول رغم كل هذا ان ارادة الحياة هي الاقوى، والا فما معنى استمرار الصراع بين قوى الظلام وقوى الشعب الذي يصر على الحياة ويرفض ان يستسلم؟ سأظل استدعي تفاؤلي، اني على يقين من ان العمر لن يمتد بي حتى اشارك في فرحة الشعب المكافح. فالدرب طويل، والوصول سوف يستغرق جيلين او ثلاثة. لنعمل ولنأمل، ان ما جاء في رسالتك الاولى عن الصحوة من الحلم المضلل الطويل ملأني جمالاً وجلالاً. احسستني كما السيدة مريم العذراء حين هتف بها جبريل: "وهزي اليك بجذع النخلة تساقط عليك رطباً جنياً" اتراني هززت بقصيدتي النخلة؟ انت يا نخلة عربية اصيلة ما احوج الامة برطبها وعطائها.

حديثك عن النباتات المائية فاقدة الجذور لم يدهشني. انتم يامن تعيشون في قلب الحضارة الاوربية المتهاوية لا مفر لكم من الشعور بالضياع والندم. هذا الشعور الذي حدثتني عنه لمسته في اعماقه كانسانة عربية لقيته هناك، واسعدني، اسعدني جداً ان اكتشف هذه الحقيقة والمس بيدي واراها بعيني. لقد اكدت لي هذه الحقيقة حقيقة اخرى هي استحالة ان يفقد الانسان العربي جذوره مهما غاب عن دياره وقومه، فالجذور تظل باقية في اغواركم البعيدة، الى هناك دائما وابدا، وانتم اذن لم يستحيل ان تقتلعه الغربة من نفوسكم حتى ولو توهمتم ذلك. فالوطن يعيش فيكم اينما كنتم، تحملونه في قلوبكم وعيونكم وحقائبكم وفي جوازات السفر، حتى لو كانت غير عربية.. قد تتغير جنسية الجواز ولكن الوجه العربي الملتصق في داخله من يستطيع ان يغير ملامحه الجميلة الاصيلة، ملامح الشمس والنخيل؟ محال.

البعد الذي قطعته عن نفسك يجعلني احبك أكثر. وها أراني احدث نفسي. لقد فقدت موهبة الحب منذ سنين – أراك تضحك. يسعدني ان تضحك – تبقت لي موهبتان: الشعر وعشق الارض الخارق

سألتني ماذا افعل في هذه الايام. أعمل على تحضير محاضرة عن "الشعر الفلسطيني" سألقيها في منتدى للشباب في "ام الفحم" وهي بلدة صغيرة في اسرائيل صادر اليهود أراضيها الخصبة وابقوا لأهلها العرب صخور الجبل. الشباب اليافع هناك ليس لديه فكرة واضحة عن شعراء فلسطين وشعرهم قبل ١٩٤٨ بسبب انقطاعهم عن الفكر العربي بحكم اوضاعهم. هم حددوا لي الموضوع وطلبوا الي ان اختم الندوة بقراءة من اشعاري

كما قلت لك في رسالة سابقة، ان رسائلي التي اكتبها اليك لا تضعك تحت طائلة الرد السريع. اكتب على مهلك وعلى مزاجك. انني احب ان اترك لأصدقائي حريتهم فلا ارهقهم بالتزامات الصارمة.

بحثت امس من عمان لأحد "قصصي" ببال عنا وقد سعدت بزيارة منه بصحبة زوجته. ولست ادري لماذا استشعرت حضورك * وكأنما هبت عليّ روائح لذيذة طيلة الجلسة.

كان عليك ان تغني الاغنية. احياناً اقول لنفسي: لعل ذوقي الموسيقي لا يزال متخلفاً وغير حضاري. اعترف انني احب الطرب والتطريب. احب الليالي والموشحات والمواويل، ولكن الظلم نفسه اذا قلت لك انني لا احب الموسيقى الغربية. واذا كنت عاجزة عن تذوقها تذوقاً عقلياً فلست بعاجزة عن تذوقها تذوقاً شعورياً. تبكيني احياناً وترهفني الى حد بعيد. ها هي انغام تشايكوفسكي في سمفونيته السادسة تأتيني خافتة ناعمة من زاوية يقبع فيها جهاز (السيكوب) قريباً مني.

ف

تُقرأ هذه الرسالة على ايقاع "المتدارك"

نابلس الارض المحتلة .
حُرِّر في اخر August / ١٩٧٠
الوقت ظهيرة يوم السبت

سامي الغالي

وصلتني منك اليوم رسالة / فيها نبضٌ فيه شعرٌ / كلماتك تورقُ، تزهرُ / تُرجع لي ذكرى الزمن الضائع من ايام العمرْ / تنسيني هذا الزمن الشائه زمن القهرْ / أتنسم فيها ريح العنبرْ / أتفيأُ ظل الشجر الأخضرْ

سامي الغالي، اما بعدُ فحالي حالي لم تتغير / الايام هنا تتشابه – ليل يعقبه فجر – / احلم فيه، اعملُ، آملُ، انتظر طلوع الفجر.. / كل الأيام سواء عندي الا يوم السبت / لو تعلم ماذا تعني لي ايام السبت / فيها يصبح للاشياء هنا في بلدي وجه مظلم / وطعم ليس يطاقْ / ومذاقٌ – ما احلى العلقم! – الصبر يلاحق من قلبي ايام السبت / اذ يهجم هذا الطوفان "الكاكيُّ" على طرقه الاسفلت / الجيش هنا وهناك يسدُّ بقلبي شريانه / يملؤني ذلاً وهواناً / يطلع في جسدي شجر المقت / ودمي يتصلب حتى الموت / يُعجزني أن ابلع ايام السبت

لو ابصرني "تمر الهندي" لكرّس من أحلى شعره.. / "وضحا" اذ ماتت ماتت معه / واعاني كأس الموت هنا في اليوم الواحد الفَ مرة / اصطبر، كم اصطبر ايام السبت / ارشف بنبال الرفض وحشرجة القلب المذبوحْ / واجدف تحت معاناتي وأئنُّ وصدري مفتوحْ : يا وطني، آهٍ، يا وطني !

هامشية :

وانا اعصر تمر الحنظل في هذي الكلمات المرّة / صوت المذياع يباغتني يخترق الصمت / يُعلن عن موجز نشرة / هذا صوت "نديم" .. بل هذا صوت "قصيّ" لكن ما بالُ اخيرا يبدو مرتبك الصوت ؟ / شيءٌ انكره في النبرة / ارهف سمعي، ماذا ؟ ماذا ؟ / [في يوم الاثنين الفاتح من سبتمبر / يجتمع الريس بلبنجر / ويتم التوقيع على.. [illegible]] وجعي، يا وجعي أخٍّ / ها انا اسقط في الفخ ../. ها انا اغرق يا سامي في نهر الوقت / من ينقذني، من ينقذني من هذا الموت /

وصية :

يا سامي استودعك الله / احفروا لي قبراً في وادٍ يُدعى وادي النسيان /
إني أتهيّأ للموت / فاطلب لي من ربي الغفران / وإذا يوما زرت ضريحي / وإذا
صليت على روحي / فاقرأ "فاتحة" النفط !

صديقتك المخلصة
فدوى طوقان

نابلس ٢٠/٩/١٩٧٣

أيها العزيز سامي

قبل أسبوعين أودعت مكتب البريد رسالتي السابقة إليك بشأن
تصوير قصائد نمر العدوان ، وقبل مغادرة المكتب توجهت الى صندوق
بريدي لأجد رسالتك في انتظاري . سرّتني المفاجأة حقاً ، ولكن
كلمات الرسالة تركت في نفسي شيئاً أكثر من السرور وأبعد أثراً .
بالنسبة لي ليس هناك شيء أجمل من ان ألتقي في درب الحياة
بإنسان يحمل في أعماقه روح شاعر ، وقد اكتشفت هذا
الشاعر فيك وانت تقرأ لي من أشعارك في تلك الأمسية
من أماسي الصيف المضيئة في لندن ، وها هي رسالتك تجيء
محمّلة بنبض الشعر لتكثّف الصورة وتضفي في جو الشعر؛
فقد كانت قصيدة حقاً، ولا أقول هذا لغواً، بدليل انها حفزتني
الى كتابة قصيدة .

يوم السبت هو يوم العطلة في اسرائيل ، يتدفق فيه الاسرائيليون
الى بلدنا المحتل ويجوبون الشوارع بحماية جنود الاحتلال ،
فيتكثف لدي الشعور بغربتي في الوطن المحتل .
حين بدأت بنظم القصيدة كنت اظن انني سأستمر في استرجاع
ذكريات الزمن الضائع من ايام العمر السحيقة ، ايام الصبا والشعر والحب؛
ولكن الذي حدث لاشعورياً ان الموضوع انقلب معي ليتحول الى
ما صارت اليه القصيدة . ما بيدي يا سامي ، انني مسكونة بموضوع

نابلس ٢٨/يوليو/١٩٧٥

ايها العزيز الصديق سامي

تحياتي واشواقي اليك. عدت الى عمان وعرفت بالأخ الصديق سليمان وشكرته على تحميله إياي رسالته الشعرية اليك والتي كانت الوسيلة الى تعارفنا عن قرب. فليس هناك أجمل من ان يلتقي الانسان بالناس الطيبين – ولا سيما الشعراء منهم – فيحس بأنه قد اغتنى واثرى بحبهم وصداقتهم. وفي الحق اني عدت من انكلترا وانا سعيدة بلقائك وبالتعرف على (الشاعر) فيك.

وحين رحلت الى نابلس اتصلت فوراً بالاستاذ احسان النمر وزرته امس مساءً حيث تحدثت اليه عن رسالتك التي تقصها عن الشاعر نمر العدوان، وحين سألته عن القصائد التي لديه قام فأتى بدفتر ضخم، او بما يسميه "سجل احسان النمر" فاذا هناك قصيدتان فقط لم تكونا جديدتين بالنسبة لي، واحدة تبدأ بالبيت: "يعقاب باب اسباب شكوانا من باب باب العذاب وباب فرقة ولدي" وقد قالها في ليلة عيد؟ اما الثانية فقد قالها يتذكر يوم اخذت وضحى نفسه للشفيله: "تذكرت يا ربي على مورد العين يا رب سالم من عيون حسدها" ومع انني على شبه يقين من انك لست في حاجة الا هاتين القصيدتين المعروفتين لنمر العدوان فقد رأيت ان انقلهما من دفتر احسان النمر واوافيك بهما لعل فيهما بعض الفائدة لك.

اما عن المئتي قصيدة التي اشار اليها المؤرخ في كتابه عن تاريخ نابلس فالرواية وردت بلسان الشيخ صالح الخفش فهذا الشيخ هو الذي كان يحفظ شعر العدوان، وانت لو رجعت الى الجزء الثاني من كتاب تاريخ جبل نابلس صفحة ٤٨٢ لوجدت في الحاشية ما يلي:

(قال لي الشيخ صالح الخفش: دونت مئتي قصيدة من شعر نمر العدوان

١٩٧٦/١/١

سامي العزيز

انظر، انت اول كلمة اكتبها. واول انسان اتحدث اليه في صباح هذا اليوم الجديد. فكل عام وقلبك مليء بالمسرة والحب والتفاؤل والامل.

في رسالتك الاخيرة تقول عن جوعك لكلماتي وتقول لي: هل من مزيد؟ هل من مزيد؟ تسألني لماذا ابخل، وتتحدث عن عطشك، وتطلب الي الا اجعلك تقف حائرا متسائلا امام باب مغلق وتقول لي: اعطنا حبا!

لن اتركك حائرا ايها العزيز. ترى هل وصلتك هديتي المرسلة بتاريخ ٢/١٦؟ انه السوار الذي تعلقت عيناك به وارجو ان تكون قد هطلت عليك بما يكفي لارواء عطشك.

لست ادري لماذا اصبحت الكتابة اليك تتطلب مني جهدا. لا بل اني ادري. فانا لست براضية عن نفسي في هذه الايام. كانت اللعنة. طريقي موحشة ومصاحبتي كئيبة. احيانا اتساءل بقسوة: لماذا نحكم آباءنا بدل من نغفر لهم؟ اليس من الجدير

بنا الآن نتحدث الى احبابنا عن غير ما هو جميل ومفرح ؟
فاذا كان وفاضنا خاليا من المفرح والجميل فلنلتزم
الصمت لكي لا نرهقهم بهذرنا الكئيب

بالمناسبة زارتني امس رفيقة لي ترجع صحبتي
لها الى ايام الطفولة. احب مصاحبة هذه الرفيقة التي
تتميز احاديثها بالصدق فلا تصدر عن ما تقول الا
عن احساس حقيقي عميق. انسانة ظلت تملك
ديناميكية عاطفية عجيبة الى ما قبل حرب حزيران،
وكنت احيانا اضيق بديناميكيتها العاطفية هذه،
وامازحها بقولي: ما هذا الانشغال الأبدي بالحب؟
او ليس في الدنيا من العذاب والمعاناة التي تقاسيها
الانسانية ما هو جدير بان يشغلنا عن الحب؟
وكانت تجيبني بكل صدق وعفوية: ثقي لو لم يوجد
في هذا العالم الا سدرة في صحراء لعشقت تلك
السدرة. تذكري يا رفيقتي اننا نستطيع ان نلخص
أمجاد الانسانية بعبارة واحدة هي: القدرة على الحب!

وكنت اقف حائرة امام جوابها ولا اعرف هل اغبطها
ام ارثي لها.

كان قانوني في الحياة، ولا يزال، هو العطاء، وسعادتي في البذل لا في الاخذ. وكان حبي لا يسترضي الا الضائع او الظمآن او الجائع. من جهة اخرى كانت العاطفة التي تغمرني نحو الآخر تحمل دائما في تركيبتها حسّ الامومة بشكل غير طبيعي. وكان حبي بسبب هذه التركيبة في عاطفتي لا يتطلب الا اقل المثوبة، كحب ام يفيض تلقائيا وينبع كمياه الانهر العذبة، وينمو، كالزهر والشجر، بقانون الطبيعة. وكان عطاؤها يذكرني دائما بعطاء حقول القمح.

في الاسابيع الاخيرة راح يبدو كأن وجهها قلق وحيرة، احسست ان هناك شيئا ما في قلبها لا تسمح له بالخروج الى السطح. وسألتها ذات يوم: ويحك ما بك؟ قالت بصوت خفيض: انني في وضع عاطفي صعب. ثم بادرتني فجأة بالسؤال عن اسم قائل هذه الابيات:

اني وقفت الى المرآة اسألها فانكرت مقلتايا كل ما رأتا
سألت اين الذي بالامس كان هنا متى ترحل عن هذا المكان متى؟
فاستجهلتني وقالت لي وما نطقت قد كان ذاك وهذا بعد ذاك أتى

قلت: الشاعر يدعى ابن زهر. قالت: تلك هي المأساة انه الخراب الذي يفعله الزمان بالانسان، اما محنة هذه المأساة فهي ان يذبل المرء بينما يبقى القلب متأججاً.

هنا توضحت لي الصورة الثانية، وعرفت سر ما تطوي من بلبلة نفسية. وقلت لها: الآن عرفت ولكن كيف حدث ذلك؟ وحكت لي القصة، وكيف بدأت من امور صغيرة جدا قد تحدث لنا كل يوم مع الانسان دون ان تترك فينا اثرا او توقظ فينا. امور لا تعني شيئاً كخروجه المفاجئ من المصعد في حركة سريعة ليستقبلها ويصحبها الى المؤسسة التي تعمل فيها. قالت: لحظتها احسست بشيء ما يشع في اجواء نفسي وكأنما اصبعاً خفية قد ضغطت على زر كهربائي في داخلي فانتشر ضوء ساطع، نور شع لحظة ثم سرعان ما اختفى عند اللقاء بالآخرين والحديث والعمل. اصر على ان نؤخذ لنا صورة معا لتنشر في مجلة المؤسسة. وانا لا احب التصوير فقلما اكون محظوظة في الصور التي تستخرج لي. وابديت عدم رغبتي ولكن الصورة اخذت لنا. واقترحت ان اعطيه واحدة

صبية وحبيبة كانت تعرض لتنشر في المجلة في حالة خروج
تلك الصورة على وجه غير مرضي ، وبحثت في حقيبة يدي
وعثرت بصورتي وقدمتها اليه ، ولكن يديه كانتا مشغولتين
بحمل بعض الادوات فأدار لي جنبه الأيسر قائلاً : ضعيها
في جيبي . وحين فعلت غمرني احساس غريب تجاهه ،
وكأن هذا الرجل اقرب الي من حبل الوريد ، واجتاحني
شعور بالحنان لا حدود له . وحين خرجنا من المؤسسة
قدم لي زجاجة عطر . وقلت لنفسي : عجباً ، كيف عرف
اني احب هذا الصنف بالذات ؟ وحين احتوتنا
السيارة اعطاني قبل ان يضع يديه على المقود
كتاباً يضم اعمال تشيكوف المسرحية . فذكرت له
انني ظللت طيلة حياتي مشدودة الى عالم دوستويفسكي
فقال انه مهتم هذه الايام بالدراما . ولم اكن قد رأيت
من مسرحيات تشيكوف الا "النورس" [illegible] قرأت
بعض قصصه القصيرة . وها انا أعود بعد حين واحن
الى تلك المجموعة من مسرحيات تشيكوف لأحيا من جديد
كأنما عرفه هذا الانسان العزيز وعاشه قبلي .
مع كل تلك الاشياء الصغيرة سقطت في اخاديد

قلبي بذرة غريبة ظللت في البداية أتجاهلها وأتغافل عنها
ولكن يبدو أن حياة الإنسان تظل محكومة بأمور صغيرة
صغيرة دون أن يكون للإرادة أو النوايا أي سلطان
عليها. فبعد عودتي إلى الوطن، ومنذ تلقيت أول
رسالة منه أخذت تلك البذرة تنمو رويداً رويداً
لتصبح شجرة عملاقة تعشش فيها الأشواق والرؤى،
ووجدتني أستجيب لنفسي شباباً أسطورياً مع كل
رسالة جديدة منه؛ ولكني ظللت أشعر في نفس
الوقت بعبثية كل هذا ولا معناه، وبدأ يجتاحني
شعور بعدم الرضى عن النفس، وبدأت أحس
بأنه علي أن أجد لي مخرجاً من هذا الحصار.

قلت لي: أنا معك في أن وضعك صعب ومثير
للتوتر والقلق، ولكن لدي فكرة. لماذا لا تتبنين
هذا الإنسان، لماذا لا تحبينه كأم. إنني أعرف
عاطفة الأمومة الفياضة التي ينطوي عليها كيانك الروحي
والجسدي. فأكدت لي أنك تحمل له كل حب أمهات الأرض
بما فيهن اللواتي [illegible] لم يلدن ولم يولدن بعد، كما
أكدت لي أن روحي بلغت من النضج المرحلة التي

تحررت نفسي من كل الأغلال المادية، وقالت: لقد علمتني الحياة
ان كل الأشياء تكتمل لتنتهي، وان كل الأشياء تنضج لتذبل
وهذه المعرفة أكسبت روحي نضجاً تسامت معه عن
الرغبات الأرضية، وانا لا ارتجي من هذا الانسان
شيئاً لنفسي. كل ما في الامر انه اضفى على
وجودي لوناً ذا نكهة ورائحة. لقد اصبح بالنسبة لي
رمزاً لشيء جميل في هذه الحياة التي غمرها الوحل
والطين حتى اختنق فيها كل جمال وخير.

تلك هي قصة رفيقتي رويتها لك فلعلك وجدت
فيها بعض المتعة بالرغم من خيط الكآبة الذي يتخللها.

لا ازال اقوم بندواتي الشعرية في مختلف مدن الضفة
وكانت آخر ندوة في مدينة الخليل. حين انتهت السهرة
ودخلت غرفة النوم المعدة لي لاحظت عدم وجود
راديو في الغرفة، فاخبرت مضيفتي ان من عادتي ان اصحو
مبكرة مهما كانت سهرتي، وانني احب الاصغاء الى نشرة
اخبار الصباح المبكرة، فوافتني بجهاز ترانزستور. لقد كنت
اتوقع سماعك في الصباح. وزهر صوتك في قلبي في ذلك
المكان الذي لم يخطر لي يوماً ان التقيك فيه.

فدوى

اني على استعداد للحصول على تصريح بزيارة يتيح لك فرصة التعرف على بلادنا واوضاعنا . واذا احببت أن تأتي برفقة الصديقة الايطالية فعلى الرحب والسعة – فربما تكون لديها رغبة في رؤية البلد الذي ينتمي اليه زوجها الـ[illegible] – على كل حال اذا رأيت أن الفكرة مقبولة وممكنة التحقيق فانني على استعداد للعمل على تحقيقها . وكل ما في الامر هو أن تشعرني بعزمك على زيارة الضفة مسبقاً وتخبرني عن الوقت المناسب والتاريخ .

لا تلزم نفسك بالرد السريع على رسائلي . فانا نفسي كسولة في كتابة الرسائل وقد انام اسابيع على رسائل الاصدقاء قبل أن أردّ عليها . لذلك كن مرتاحاً من هذه الناحية ، ولا بأس عليك .

لك أصدق المودة واخلص مشاعر الصداقة وليحفظك الله .

المخلصة
فدوى طوقان

Photographs of Fadwa Tuqan with Sami Haddad in London

BOOK REVIEWS OF *Fadwa Tuqan's Letters to Thurayya Haddad*

"This book reviews letters written by Fadwa Tuqan to her friend Thurayya Haddad. The letters were introduced by Moroccan poet Abdel Latif Alwarari and were prepared for publication by Samir Haddad. In its first edition, the book presents various aspects of the poet's life and her social relations. The letters also expose the private life of poet Fadwa Tuqan, one hundred years after her birth, and her connection to the world around her. It sheds a new light on her life and poetry. This book also contains samples of letters written by poet Fadwa Tuqan."

Palestinian News and Information Agency

"This exciting book sheds light on the life of an exceptional poet; exceptional in her pioneering poetry, as she was the first female Palestinian woman poet in the twentieth century. Fadwa Tuqan is important, as she was among the first to break free from the cocoon of social taboos with no religious, ethical or legal basis and to suffer greatly as a result of the occupation and at the hands of family and society."

Labeeb Faleh Taha, Al-Mayadeen, February 1, 2018

In 2017, Moroccan poetic and critic Abdel Latif Alwarari received a similar gift and a trove that is no less if not more important than what Rajaa' Al-Naqqash. The letters Al-Naqqash received were from one side, which is Anwar Al-Ma'adawi, as Fadwa's letters disappeared in conditions that we will detail later on. But what Alwarari received were letters written by Fadwa herself, and it is a real trove, not just in light of the rarity of personal documents related to the extremely cautious and secretive Fadwa, but also because of the information and stories that shed significant light on the life of Fadwa Tuqan and her creativity...

Osama Farouq, Akhbar Al-Adab, January 19, 2018

"In these letters, the mother of Palestinian poetry exposes deep personal confessions, a true and sincere revelation about the difficulties and spiritual bruises she sustained in her life, blending her personal concerns with those of her occupied homeland, especially that most of these letters were written after the 1967 defeat, leading up to the Palestinian intifada. All in all, these are thirty letters of pain, alienation and void, and perhaps desperation."

Khalil Sweileh, Al-Akhbar, November 24, 2018

www.ingramcontent.com/pod-product-compliance
Lightning Source LLC
Chambersburg PA
CBHW031307120726
47906CB00003B/933
* 9 7 8 0 9 9 6 8 9 3 3 9 8 *